Beesola
the
Happy Bee

Written
by

Tolu Akintola

Beesola

That friend who is always happy at all times;
always singing and is a shoulder to lean on in hard times.

She is the friend who accepts everyone.
She never judges.
She always wants the best for everyone.

Special thanks to Wonu, Timi, Oyin and Toluwani.

This amazing book
belongs to:

Beesola is a very happy bee.

Home is where the honey is

She lives in a hive,
in a beautiful garden.

The garden has lots of trees,
a happy bunny
and many flowers.

Every morning,
the sun comes out
and shines very bright.

Each day,
Beesola and her friends

come out to play.

How many friends can you see?

Beesola loves to play
with the flowers.
They give her pollen
to make honey.

HONEY

Beesola loves to make honey.

She gave some to Bambor,

the big brown bear

who lives in the wood.

One morning,
Beesola looked in the mirror.
She saw her image.
"I am the same everyday!"
She said.

Home is where the honey is

She became sad.
"Why can't I be like my friends?"
She asked herself.

"Oh! I know what to do.
I will put on glitters like
Basira the butterfly,
and I will be happy again."

So, Beesola put a lot of gold glitter on her body and she was shining very bright.

She called out to her friends
to come and play but no one came.
They were afraid of the
shiny flying object.

They ran into
the little mushroom house
and would not come out.

"Oh dear," Beesola said, "I guess shiny things can't make everybody happy. I will have to be someone else.

"Fiyin the firefly is always happy.
He brings light to everybody.
I want to be just like Fiyin"

So, Beesola bought three
buckets of paint.
She painted herself in blue,
orange and yellow;
just like Fiyin the firefly.

She went to the flowers.
She wanted some pollen to
make honey. The flowers did not
know it was Beesola. They were
hiding in the leaves.

Beesola was very sad.
She had no friends.
She had no pollen,
and she had no honey.

Then she remembered the twins, Lara and Lola the Ladybirds. They are so beautiful and they always seem to have lots of fun.

So, Beesola made a red dress for herself. She puts some black polka dots on it. She also bought a pair of black boots.

Then, she put on the dress
and the pair of boots.
"Now, I hope I will be as happy
as Lara and Lola," she said.

Off to the colony of bees,
Beesola went, to borrow
some honey. She was wearing
her new polka dot dress and boots.

The Queen's Hive

"What is that?" A bee screamed as Beesola approached. Some bees were afraid, some were confused; only the baby bee was excited.

The Queen's Hive

"Run!!! It's a beebug!" shouted Beedemi, the smart bee.

The Queen's Hive

"Dont be silly," Baba, the old bee replied. "It's just a red fly coming to take our honey. We must fight it."

The Queen's Hive

The cool bee, Beesi, was amused. "Finally, the aliens are coming, one at a time," he said.

The Queen's Hive

All the bees were hiding, except
Beebee the baby bee.
He was excited.
"This is a new toy", he said.

The Queen's Hive

The queen, Beesoye came out of her hive. "Hello! What are you and what do you want from us?" she asked.

The Queen's Hive

"It is me, Beesola."
Beesola replied the queen.
Then, she told the queen how
she tried to be the butterfly,
the firefly and the ladybirds.

The Queen's Hive

"And now, I have lost everything."
Beesola sobbed.
"I have no friends. I have no family.
I have no honey to give the bear.
I don't know who I am anymore!"

The Queen's Hive

"Don't bee silly,"
Queen Beesoye said,
"You can be only the best version
of yourself. No one can be you
and you cannot be someone else."

The Queen's Hive

"Think about how you were before the change; think about the things you like and the things that made you happy."

"Thank you", Beesola said.
She quickly flew back to her hive.
She took off the polka dot dress
and the boots.

She looked into the mirror and said to herself:

"I am unique. No one else can be me except me. I can only be a better version of myself."

With a big smile, Beesola flew
out of her hive and called
to her friends:
"Come out and play."

After peeping through the windows, all Beesola's friends came out to play. Even Bambor, the big brown bear joined in the games.

Beesola's family also came to play.
The flowers blossom and
gave lots of pollen.
Everybody was happy and
all felt loved.

I am special.
I am unique.
No one else can be me.

That night, Beesola put a new
sign on her wall.
Then, she went to bed and had a
peaceful sleep;
a very happy bee.

Now, it's your turn.

This is me

My name: _______________________________

What makes me happy: _______________

____

What people like about me: __________

____

Say to yourself:

I am unique.
I am special.
I cannot be anybody else.
Nobody can be me.
I can only be the best version of myself.

Thank you for your purchase.

If you are happy with your book,
please support us and leave a review.
On Amazon, go to Customer Reviews section
on the book detail page and click

"Write a customer review"

We appreciate your positive feedback
and constructive suggestions to improve our services.
We hope others will be able to benefit from your review.

Thank you.

Tolu Akintola
(Beesola's friend)